Amelia Earhart

by Jonatha A. Brown

Reading consultant: Susan Nations, M.Ed., author/literacy coach/consultant

WR WEEKLY READER

EARLY LEARNING LIBRARY

Please visit our web site at: www.earlyliteracy.cc
For a free color catalog describing Weekly Reader® Early Learning Library's list
of high-quality books, call 1-877-445-5824 (USA) or 1-800-387-3178 (Canada).
Weekly Reader® Early Learning Library's fax: (414) 336-0164.

Library of Congress Cataloging-in-Publication Data

Brown, Jonatha A.
    Amelia Earhart / by Jonatha A. Brown.
      p. cm. — (People we should know)
    Includes bibliographical references and index.
    ISBN 0-8368-4465-3 (lib. bdg.)
    ISBN 0-8368-4472-6 (softcover)
    1. Earhart, Amelia, 1897-1937—Juvenile literature. 2. Women air pilots—United States—Biography—
Juvenile literature. 3. Air pilots—United States—Biography—Juvenile literature. I. Title. II. Series.
TL540.E3B748   2005
629.13'092—dc22
  [B]
                                                                         2004057249

This edition first published in 2005 by
Weekly Reader® Early Learning Library
330 West Olive Street, Suite 100
Milwaukee, WI 53212 USA

Copyright © 2005 by Weekly Reader® Early Learning Library

Based on *Amelia Earhart* (Trailblazers of the Modern World series) by Lucia Raatma
Editor: JoAnn Early Macken
Designer: Scott M. Krall
Picture researcher: Diane Laska-Swanke

Photo credits: Cover, title © Topical Press Agency/Getty Images; p. 4 © Getty Images; pp. 5, 10, 18, 19, 20
© AP/Wide World Photos; p. 7 © Sasha/Getty Images; p. 9 © APA/Getty Images; p. 11 © Keystone/Hulton
Archive/Getty Images; p. 13 © American Stock/Getty Images; p. 15 © J. Gaiger/Topical Press Agency/
Getty Images; p. 17 © Hulton Archive/Getty Images

Printed in the United States of America

1 2 3 4 5 6 7 8 9 09 08 07 06 05

Table of Contents

Words that appear in the glossary are printed in **boldface**
type the first time they occur in the text.

Chapter 1: Growing Up

Amelia Mary Earhart was born on July 24, 1897. She lived in Kansas with her parents and her sister Muriel. Amelia's grandparents lived nearby. They often took care of the girls.

Amelia and Muriel were not just sisters. They were best friends, too. They both liked to play outdoors. For them, playing ball was more fun than playing quietly in the house. They lived near the Mississippi River. The bank of the river was a fine place to play. The girls caught

Amelia and her sister Muriel liked to play outdoors. Amelia is holding the toy dog.

Amelia's home life was not always fun. Her father had problems. He could not keep a job for long. Finally, his wife left him. She and the girls moved to Chicago. The move was hard on Amelia. She missed her father. She wanted her family to be whole again.

After the move, Amelia changed. She kept to herself. She did not spend much time with groups of children. She worked hard in school and studied a lot. She followed her own path.

Adventure Again

In 1917, Amelia was twenty years old. She felt grown up, and she wanted to be on her own. She also wanted to go away to college. She left home and went to school near Philadelphia. There she met many new people. She took all kinds of classes. She worked, too. In her free time, she rode horses and played tennis. To Amelia, it all seemed to be an adventure. Doing new things was fun.

fish. They went exploring. Amelia and her sister liked **adventure**!

Some people thought the girls were too active. Some people thought they acted more like boys. Back then, most girls were taught to be quiet and gentle. But the Earharts did not raise their daughters that way. They wanted their girls to be active and **curious**.

Th
w
w

As Amelia grew up, she kept trying new things.

Amelia visited Muriel in Canada. There, she saw men who had been fighting in a war. Some of them were badly hurt. Amelia wanted to help. The next year, she became a nurse's helper. She took care of soldiers who had been hurt. After the war ended, she thought she wanted to be a doctor. She went back to school in New York.

Chapter 2: Learning to Fly

While Amelia was away, her parents got back together. They moved to California. Amelia went for a visit. On that trip, her father took her to an air show. It was the first air show she had ever seen. Planes flew overhead. The pilots did stunts. The show was fun to watch.

A New Dream

This show gave Amelia an idea. She would go up in a plane. A few days later, she did just that. She paid a pilot to take her flying. The flight lasted only ten minutes, but that was long enough. In those few minutes, Amelia changed her mind. She forgot about being a doctor. She had to learn to fly!

In those days, most people thought flying a plane was a job for a man. They thought women should

Women earned the right to vote in 1920. Yet many people still did not think women should fly.

take care of their homes. They should raise children. Some could be **secretaries**, nurses, or teachers. But they should leave flying to men.

Amelia did not care what people thought. She stayed in California. She signed up for flying lessons. Then she got a job at a phone company to pay for them. She worked hard all week and went flying on weekends.

Dressed for Work

When she flew a plane, Amelia dressed like a man. Some people thought she should wear a skirt and nice shoes. Amelia knew that a skirt would get in a pilot's way. Ladies' shoes would get dirty. She needed to wear pants and boots. She also needed **goggles** and a leather jacket. She dressed in a way that made sense for pilots.

In 1922, Amelia earned her pilot's license. At last, she could fly a plane by herself. At the time, she was one of only a few female pilots in the world.

Amelia had to learn how to control an airplane.

Chapter 3: Moving to Boston

By this time, Amelia had her own plane. But she could not find work as a pilot. No one would pay a woman to fly a plane. To earn money, she had to do "women's work."

Amelia's parents **divorced** in the 1920s. After that, her mother and Muriel decided to move. They wanted to live in Boston. Amelia wanted to go with them. So she sold her plane. She used the money to buy a car. Then she drove all the way to Boston.

Driving from California to Boston

Cars did not go very fast in 1926. Many roads were not very good. Amelia's trip took quite a while. All that was okay with her. She still liked adventure!

Amelia spent as much time in a plane as she could.

In Boston, Amelia found a job. She worked with children and taught English to people from other countries. She also joined a pilot's group. She flew planes when she could.

A Chance to Be First

One day, she received a phone call from a stranger. His name was Hilton Railey. He had a question for Amelia. Would she like to fly across the Atlantic Ocean? No other woman had ever done such a thing. The flight would be a first. Amelia liked the idea very much. She thought it could be a fine adventure. So she said yes.

Amelia was excited about the flight. Then she learned that she was to be **commander** of the flight. She was not going to fly the plane. Instead, two men were going to share the pilot's job. Amelia was disappointed. Even so, she wanted to go.

Hilton Railey and Amelia were excited about her trip across the ocean.

Chapter 4: Flying High

On June 3, 1928, Amelia and the two pilots climbed into the plane. They took off from Boston. First, they flew north to Newfoundland. There they took on more fuel. They hoped it would be enough to fly across the ocean.

The flyers had planned to leave right away. Suddenly, however, the weather turned bad. They had to wait for clear skies. Two weeks passed.

Across the Atlantic

Finally, on June 17, the weather was good. The three climbed back into the plane and took off. They headed east. The trip had begun. The flight started out well. Then night came. Suddenly, the radio in the plane stopped working. They kept going, but they did not know exactly where they were. The next morning, the ocean was still below them. They were almost out of fuel. But then they spotted land. The plane soon touched down in Wales. They had made it!

Amelia told the story of her flight over and over again.

That flight made Amelia famous. The two men who had flown the plane got less attention. Men had made long flights before, but women had not. Many people wanted to hear about her trip. They paid Amelia to give talks and write a book about it.

With the money she earned, Amelia bought a new plane. Then she flew it back and forth across the country. On that trip, she flew **solo** — no one was with her. That was another first for a woman.

George Putnam did not try to change Amelia. He liked her adventurous spirit.

In 1931, Amelia married George Putnam. He knew Amelia loved adventure. He knew she would not want to stay at home. George was right. After they

Cheering crowds greeted Amelia as she finished her solo flight across the ocean.

married, Amelia kept flying. She still gave talks, too. She often told women that they could do many of the things men were doing.

The next year, Amelia flew across the Atlantic again. This time, though, she was the pilot, and she was flying solo. It was a tough flight. The plane had a few problems, and she flew into a storm. In the end, she reached land safely. She was the first woman to make that long trip alone.

Amelia and her copilot looked relaxed before their last flight.

Over the next few years, she set more records. Then she decided to fly around the world. It would be a **risky** trip. Some people said it would be too risky. Amelia did not agree. She was sure she could do it. She hired a few men to help her. Then she started making plans for the flight.

Her first try began in March 1937. She and one of the men took off from California.

They flew to Hawaii and refueled. Then they had a problem. The plane did not go fast enough to take off. Amelia lost control, and the landing gear broke. The plane had to be fixed. The trip had to wait.

Missing

She tried again on June 1. Amelia and a second pilot were on the plane. No one else was onboard. They flew day after day, stopping often for fuel. On June 30, they reached the island of New Guinea. They refueled and took off again. They headed for Howland Island, a tiny island in the Pacific Ocean.

No one knows what went wrong, but Amelia never reached that island. When her plane did not arrive on time, a search began. Nothing was ever found. The plane was gone. The copilot was gone. Amelia was gone. It is a **mystery** that has never been solved.

Glossary

adventure — exciting or dangerous feat

commander — person in charge

curious — interested in learning more about something

divorced — ended a marriage

goggles — glasses that fit close to the face and are worn to protect the eyes

mystery — something that is not known or cannot be understood

risky — filled with danger

secretaries — workers who write letters and manage office work for their employers

solo — alone

For More Information

Books

Amelia Earhart. Rookie Biographies (series). Wil Mara (Children's Press)

A Picture Book of Amelia Earhart. Picture Book Biography (series). David A. Adler (Holiday House)

Vanished! The Mysterious Disappearance of Amelia Earhart. Step into Reading (series). Monica Kulling (Random House)

The Wright Brothers. People to Know (series). Jonatha A. Brown (Gareth Stevens)

Web Sites

Amelia Earhart Birthplace Museum

www.ameliaearhartmuseum.org/index.html

Information, fun facts, pictures, and more

The Official Site of Amelia Earhart

www.ameliaearhart.com/

Another good place to learn more about this brave woman

Women Who Changed History

www.teacher.scholastic.com/activities/women/index.htm

Information about Amelia Earhart and other famous women

Index

About the Author

Jonatha A. Brown has written several books for children. She lives in Phoenix, Arizona, with her husband and two dogs. If you happen to come by when she isn't at home working on a book, she's probably out riding or visiting with one of her horses. She may be gone for quite a while, so you'd better come back later.